This book belongs to....

Made in the USA
Columbia, SC
08 December 2022

72929529R00067